Quilter's
DESK DIARY
2013

Welcome to 2013

Stay organized in style with *The Quilter's Desk Diary 2013*. Illustrated throughout with beautiful photographs of inspirational quilts from the most talented of quiltmakers, each week-to-view diary page has plenty of room for your own personal notes. If you want to find out more about any of the quiltmakers featured, turn to the back of the book for information about them and the books they have written.

David and Charles
www.rucraft.co.uk

Fridays child is loving and giving.

31
Monday

Starting the year as a new Gran to Gabriel David born 28th Dec ½ past midnight weighing 6lb 4oz.

New Year's Day

1
Tuesday

Travelled to Sheffield to see Gabriel

2
Wednesday

Off to ASE

3
Thursday

4
Friday

5
Saturday

Return from ASE full of cold.

6
Sunday

Garden Walk

Why not make a New Year's resolution that this will be the year you enter a quilting competition? You may be as lucky as Laura Coons, who, although she had been quilting for just three years, won 1st prize in the 2011 Jelly Roll Dream Challenge. All the competition's winning quilts can be seen in *Jelly Roll Dreams*, compiled by Pam and Nicky Lintott.

DECEMBER						
M	T	W	T	F	S	S
					1	2
3	4	5	6	7	8	9
10	11	12	13	14	15	16
17	18	19	20	21	22	23
24	25	26	27	(28)	29	30
31						

January

7
Monday

8
Tuesday

9
Wednesday

10
Thursday

11
Friday

12
Saturday

13
Sunday

Peace Medallion
This colourful design by Paula Diggle appears in *Jelly Roll Inspirations*, a collection of quilt patterns compiled by Pam and Nicky Lintott, selected from the 2009 Jelly Roll Challenge competition.

			JANUARY			
M	T	W	T	F	S	S
	1	2	3	4	5	6
7	8	9	10	11	12	13
14	15	16	17	18	19	20
21	22	23	24	25	26	27
28	29	30	31			

January

14
Monday

15
Tuesday

16
Wednesday

17
Thursday

Lots of snow.

18
Friday

Travelled to Sheffield despite snow
to visit Gabriel + chaos trio meeting.

19
Saturday

20
Sunday

Floral Dimensions

Pauline Ineson's award-winning floral appliqué quilt has collected
many coveted prizes both in the UK (at Quilts UK and Festival of
Quilts) and in the US (at the AQS and IQS shows). In her book,
Floral Dimensions, she explains how to make 20 stunning 3D flowers,
just like those featured on the quilt, using a range of machine
appliqué techniques.

			JANUARY			
M	T	W	T	F	S	S
	1	2	3	4	5	6
7	8	9	10	11	12	13
14	15	16	17	18	19	20
21	22	23	24	25	26	27
28	29	30	31			

January

Martin Luther King Day (US)

21
Monday

22
Tuesday

23
Wednesday

24
Thursday

25
Friday

Australia Day (Aus)

26
Saturday

27
Sunday

Marumon Screen

In *Japanese Sashiko Inspirations* Susan Briscoe has created stylish projects to explore the decorative possibilities of sashiko, the traditional technique of using lines of simple running stitch to create striking patterns on fabric. Circular designs called *marumon* are considered unique to Japanese design, and this impressive screen would bring a stylish touch to any room.

JANUARY

M	T	W	T	F	S	S
	1	2	3	4	5	6
7	8	9	10	11	12	13
14	15	16	17	18	19	20
21	22	23	24	25	26	27
28	29	30	31			

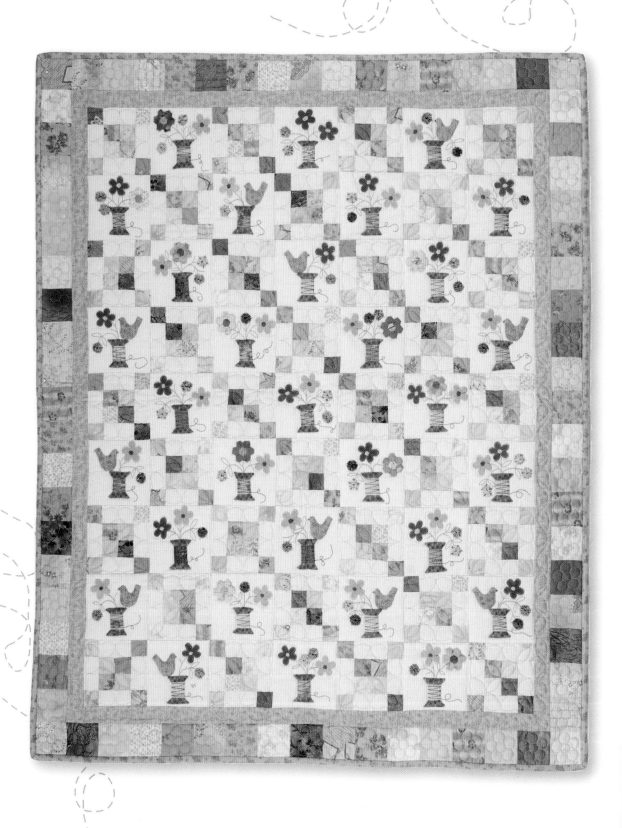

28
Monday

29
Tuesday

30
Wednesday

31
Thursday

1
Friday

2
Saturday

3
Sunday

Flower Spool
This delightful antique-style quilt from Lynette Anderson's
Country Cottage Quilting uses her distinctive palette of soft and
faded colours. Texture and dimension are created with English
paper pieced hexagons and yoyo flowers.

			JANUARY			
M	T	W	T	F	S	S
	1	2	3	4	5	6
7	8	9	10	11	12	13
14	15	16	17	18	19	20
21	22	23	24	25	26	27
28	29	30	31			

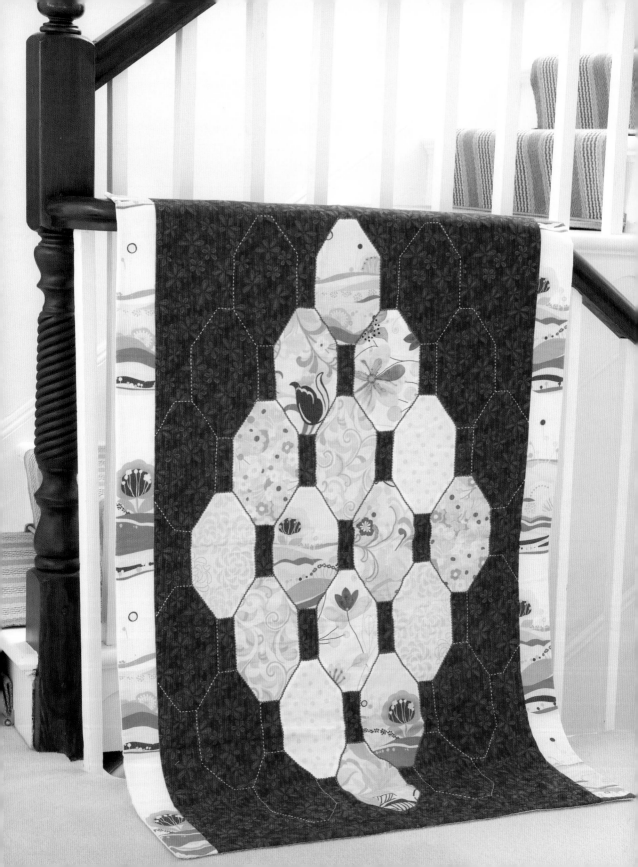

February

4
Monday

5
Tuesday

6
Wednesday

7
Thursday

8
Friday

9
Saturday

Chinese New Year

10
Sunday

Chinese Lanterns

The lanterns on this pretty wall hanging are made using the technique of English paper piecing, then appliquéd onto an Oriental-themed background fabric. The lantern's octagonal shape was used again for the hand quilting. English paper piecing is just one of over 220 patchwork, quilting and appliqué techniques explored in *The Quilter's Bible* by Linda Clements.

		FEBRUARY				
M	T	W	T	F	S	S
				1	2	3
4	5	6	7	8	9	10
11	12	13	14	15	16	17
18	19	20	21	22	23	24
25	26	27	28			

February

11
Monday

Shrove Tuesday

12
Tuesday

13
Wednesday

Valentine's Day

14
Thursday

15
Friday

16
Saturday

17
Sunday

Loving Hearts

This quilt, which features in *Two From One Jelly Roll Quilts* by Pam and
Nicky Lintott, is the perfect way to show someone how much you care.
Made from delicate pastel fabrics, the blocks are set on point and framed
with narrow sashing strips, so that the hearts really stand out. A scrolling
heart design has been longarm quilted across the finished quilt.

FEBRUARY

M	T	W	T	F	S	S
				1	2	3
4	5	6	7	8	9	10
11	12	13	14	15	16	17
18	19	20	21	22	23	24
25	26	27	28			

February

Presidents' Day (US)

18
Monday

19
Tuesday

20
Wednesday

21
Thursday

22
Friday

23
Saturday

24
Sunday

Little Rocking Horse

There is no better reason to give a handmade gift than the birth of a baby. *Quilt a Gift for Little Ones* by Barri Sue Gaudet (Bareroots) has over 20 projects to welcome the newest addition to the family, from simple crib decorations to keepsake quilts. The centre panel of this cot quilt is decorated with an appliquéd rocking horse and is bordered by alternating Star and Square-Within-a-Square blocks.

FEBRUARY

M	T	W	T	F	S	S
				1	2	3
4	5	6	7	8	9	10
11	12	13	14	15	16	17
18	19	20	21	22	23	24
25	26	27	28			

25
Monday

26
Tuesday

27
Wednesday

28
Thursday

1
Friday

2
Saturday

3
Sunday

Daffodil Dimensions
The daffodil is the national flower of Wales, which is very fitting as the Welsh celebrate St David's Day this week (1st March). This block shows a detail from Pauline Ineson's Floral Dimensions quilt, and in the book of the same name, Pauline describes how to make 20 dimensional flowers including both the daffodil and the pink carnations pictured here.

		FEBRUARY				
M	T	W	T	F	S	S
				1	2	3
4	5	6	7	8	9	10
11	12	13	14	15	16	17
18	19	20	21	22	23	24
25	26	27	28			

4
Monday

5
Tuesday

6
Wednesday

7
Thursday

8
Friday

9
Saturday

Mother's Day (UK)

10
Sunday

Lovin' That Muffin

Amateur quilter Claire Hepworth won 4th place in the 2011 Jelly Roll Dream Challenge with this, the first Jelly Roll™ quilt she ever made. Entrants had to make their quilt designs using just one Jelly Roll™ plus a limited allowance of extra fabric. The competition attracted contributions from all over the world and the winning quilt designs can be seen in *Jelly Roll Dreams*.

			MARCH			
M	T	W	T	F	S	S
				1	2	3
4	5	6	7	8	9	10
11	12	13	14	15	16	17
18	19	20	21	22	23	24
25	26	27	28	29	30	31

March

11
Monday

12
Tuesday

13
Wednesday

14
Thursday

15
Friday

16
Saturday

St Patrick's Day

17
Sunday

Celtic Sampler Quilt

In her elegant wall hanging, Daphne Green has reinterpreted some of the blocks featured in *The Essential Sampler Quilt Book* by Lynne Edwards, adding beautiful Celtic motifs to the centre panel. Lynne's book has masterclass instruction for making 40 blocks using both hand and machine techniques so you too can make an heirloom sampler quilt.

MARCH

M	T	W	T	F	S	S
				1	2	3
4	5	6	7	8	9	10
11	12	13	14	15	16	17
18	19	20	21	22	23	24
25	26	27	28	29	30	31

March

18
Monday

19
Tuesday

20
Wednesday

21
Thursday

22
Friday

23
Saturday

24
Sunday

			MARCH			
M	T	W	T	F	S	S
				1	2	3
4	5	6	7	8	9	10
11	12	13	14	15	16	17
18	19	20	21	22	23	24
25	26	27	28	29	30	31

Fantasy Flowers

Pam and Nicky Lintott are expert at helping quilters to get the most from all their favourite pre-cut fabric bundles. This quilt, with its combination of spiralling inner flower blocks and Sawtooth-bordered outer flower blocks, is just one of 14 designs featured in their book, *More Layer Cake, Jelly Roll & Charm Quilts*.

25
Monday

26
Tuesday

27
Wednesday

28
Thursday

Good Friday (UK, Aus)

29
Friday

30
Saturday

Easter Sunday

31
Sunday

Spring Chickens

Grace the Easter table with this cute table mat with its simple foundation-pieced chickens decorated with a little felt appliqué and hand embroidery. Continue the theme with a chicken doorstop. These are just two of the ideas to be found in Mandy Shaw's *Quilt Yourself Gorgeous,* which is full of ideas for using your sewing skills to bring a personal touch to your home.

			MARCH			
M	T	W	T	F	S	S
				1	2	3
4	5	6	7	8	9	10
11	12	13	14	15	16	17
18	19	20	21	22	23	24
25	26	27	28	29	30	31

April

1
Monday

2
Tuesday

3
Wednesday

4
Thursday

5
Friday

6
Saturday

7
Sunday

Cherry Blossoms

Joanna Figueroa, founder of Fig Tree & Co and publisher of
over 100 patterns, was inspired to create this quilt design by the
spring blossoms outside her kitchen window. The simple pieced
background gives the appliqué project added depth and movement.
Joanna's quilt designs have a soft, vintage look about them, updated
with clean, fresh colours. A colour masterclass from this talented
designer is featured in *The Quiltmakers*.

			APRIL			
M	T	W	T	F	S	S
1	2	3	4	5	6	7
8	9	10	11	12	13	14
15	16	17	18	19	20	21
22	23	24	25	26	27	28
29	30					

April

8
Monday

9
Tuesday

10
Wednesday

11
Thursday

12
Friday

13
Saturday

14
Sunday

My Favourite Garden

This super little wall quilt from Lynette Anderson's *Country Cottage Quilting* celebrates the joys of the garden. Nine delightful scenes combine appliqué with hand embroidery. The blocks are framed by narrow strips of fabric in a Courthouse Steps pattern, with a simple border of pieced rectangles to finish. A variety of hand-painted buttons from Lynette Anderson Designs add dimension and texture.

APRIL

M	T	W	T	F	S	S
1	2	3	4	5	6	7
8	9	10	11	12	13	14
15	16	17	18	19	20	21
22	23	24	25	26	27	28
29	30					

15
Monday

16
Tuesday

17
Wednesday

18
Thursday

19
Friday

20
Saturday

21
Sunday

Lollipop Flowers

Clare Kingslake's *Folk Quilt Appliqué* is a book devoted to providing quilters with ways to make quilts using appliqué. Fields of flowers are the theme of this quilt; small hexagons made with English paper piecing create the green centre, with appliquéd lollipop flowers surrounding them. The background is heavily embroidered in French knots, adding texture and detail. A pieced border of triangles, made easy with foundation piecing, is embroidered with stippling, while a third border frames the quilt nicely.

APRIL						
M	T	W	T	F	S	S
1	2	3	4	5	6	7
8	9	10	11	12	13	14
15	16	17	18	19	20	21
22	23	24	25	26	27	28
29	30					

April

22
Monday

23
Tuesday

24
Wednesday

25
Thursday

26
Friday

27
Saturday

28
Sunday

Ranru Wall Hanging

Susan Briscoe is an expert in sashiko stitching, having learnt the techique from traditional needlewomen when living in Japan. In *Japanese Sashiko Inspirations* she explores new and innovative ways to use sashiko patterns to create stylish projects to complement the modern home. The simple piecing of this little wall hanging focuses the attention on the lovely stitched samples.

APRIL

M	T	W	T	F	S	S
1	2	3	4	5	6	7
8	9	10	11	12	13	14
15	16	17	18	19	20	21
22	23	24	25	26	27	28
29	30					

29
Monday

30
Tuesday

1
Wednesday

2
Thursday

3
Friday

4
Saturday

5
Sunday

APRIL						
M	T	W	T	F	S	S
1	2	3	4	5	6	7
8	9	10	11	12	13	14
15	16	17	18	19	20	21
22	23	24	25	26	27	28
29	30					

Blossom Time

Bring a touch of the country cottage into your home with this charming vintage-style quilt. This is just one of 17 stunning designs featured in *Layer Cake, Jelly Roll and Charm Quilts* by Pam and Nicky Lintott, a book that is dedicated to providing ingenious ideas for using pre-cut fabric collections with little or no waste.

May

Bank Holiday (UK)

6
Monday

7
Tuesday

8
Wednesday

9
Thursday

10
Friday

11
Saturday

Mother's Day (US, Aus)

12
Sunday

High Fashion

This quilt is made up of 20 Handbag blocks that make excellent
use of the large squares in a layer cake, so it is very quick to piece.
It took quiltmaker Ellen Seward just two hours! The handles are
appliquéd on by hand, although machine appliqué would speed
things up. This lovely design features in Pam and Nicky Lintott's
More Layer Cake, Jelly Roll & Charm Quilts.

			MAY			
M	T	W	T	F	S	S
		1	2	3	4	5
6	7	8	9	10	11	12
13	14	15	16	17	18	19
20	21	22	23	24	25	26
27	28	29	30	31		

13
Monday

14
Tuesday

15
Wednesday

16
Thursday

17
Friday

18
Saturday

19
Sunday

The Patchwork Village

There is nothing Mandy Shaw likes better than making things for the home and in *Stitch at Home*, she presents a gorgeous collection of designs to brighten up your house in her own unmistakeable style. This patchwork quilt, with its easy pieced block and simple appliqué shapes, gave her the chance to create a whole village in fabric!

MAY

M	T	W	T	F	S	S
		1	2	3	4	5
6	7	8	9	10	11	12
13	14	15	16	17	18	19
20	21	22	23	24	25	26
27	28	29	30	31		

May

20
Monday

21
Tuesday

22
Wednesday

23
Thursday

24
Friday

25
Saturday

26
Sunday

A Gathering of Geishas

A bold fabric panel featuring geisha figures superimposed over
Mount Fuji, with a design of birds and flowers in the printed frame
border, is the central focus of this colourful quilt by Susan Briscoe
(*Japanese Quilt Inspirations*). With so much going on, all that was
required was a simple strip border made from scrap fabrics selected
to pick out the vibrant colours of the central picture.

			MAY			
M	T	W	T	F	S	S
		1	2	3	4	5
6	7	8	9	10	11	12
13	14	15	16	17	18	19
20	21	22	23	24	25	26
27	28	29	30	31		

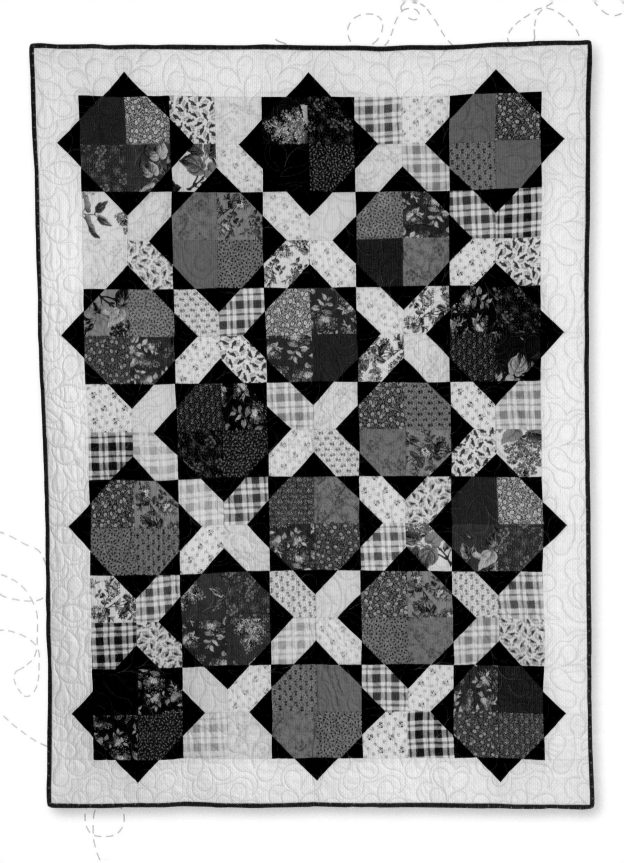

May

Memorial Day (US)
Spring Bank Holiday (UK)

27
Monday

28
Tuesday

29
Wednesday

30
Thursday

31
Friday

1
Saturday

2
Sunday

Four-Patch Flip

The success of this charm quilt is dependant on choosing fabrics to ensure that the stars surrounding the dark Four-Patch blocks stand out. Creating contrast between the blocks is essential, so choose a charm pack with a good selection of lights and darks. *More Layer Cake, Jelly Roll & Charm Quilts* has many more pre-cut fabric quilts from Pam and Nicky Lintott.

MAY

M	T	W	T	F	S	S
		1	2	3	4	5
6	7	8	9	10	11	12
13	14	15	16	17	18	19
20	21	22	23	24	25	26
27	28	29	30	31		

June

3
Monday

4
Tuesday

5
Wednesday

6
Thursday

7
Friday

8
Saturday

9
Sunday

Feathered Friends

This gorgeous quilt from Clare Kingslake's *Folk Quilt Appliqué* is filled with birds, flowers and leaves appliquéd onto brushed cotton. There are flashes of bright blues, pinks and yellows, and the detail is achieved by needle felting, machine embroidery and machine quilting with a doodling floral design. There are seven blocks repeated in a reverse layout for a visually stunning piece.

JUNE

M	T	W	T	F	S	S
					1	2
3	4	5	6	7	8	9
10	11	12	13	14	15	16
17	18	19	20	21	22	23
24	25	26	27	28	29	30

June

10
Monday

11
Tuesday

12
Wednesday

13
Thursday

14
Friday

15
Saturday

Father's Day (US, UK)

16
Sunday

			JUNE			
M	T	W	T	F	S	S
					1	2
3	4	5	6	7	8	9
10	11	12	13	14	15	16
17	18	19	20	21	22	23
24	25	26	27	28	29	30

Star Sampler
A taupe Jelly Roll™ was the starting point for this elegant sampler quilt, which features in Pam and Nicky Lintott's book, *Jelly-Roll Sampler Quilts*. Nine variations of the popular Star block were used in the design in three different sizes.

June

17
Monday

18
Tuesday

19
Wednesday

20
Thursday

21
Friday

22
Saturday

23
Sunday

Pac-Mania

Angelika Sins' quilt won 2nd prize in the 2011 Jelly Roll
Dream Challenge. Her design is an adaptation of the traditional
Grandmother's Fan block, which allows larger pieces of fabric to
be shown and brings out the colourful batiks nicely. Don't let the
curved seams discourage you – it's easier than it looks!

JUNE						
M	T	W	T	F	S	S
					1	2
3	4	5	6	7	8	9
10	11	12	13	14	15	16
17	18	19	20	21	22	23
24	25	26	27	28	29	30

24
Monday

25
Tuesday

26
Wednesday

27
Thursday

28
Friday

29
Saturday

30
Sunday

Yo-Yo Roses

Fabric yo-yos in deep reds and pinks are used to represent roses in this special little quilt, with appliquéd leaves and embroidered tendrils completing the effect. You can make the quilt larger or smaller as you please, simpling by adding more blocks or taking some away. This is just one of 25 heart-felt projects featured in Barri Sue Gaudet's *Quilt a Gift*.

			JUNE			
M	T	W	T	F	S	S
					1	2
3	4	5	6	7	8	9
10	11	12	13	14	15	16
17	18	19	20	21	22	23
24	25	26	27	28	29	30

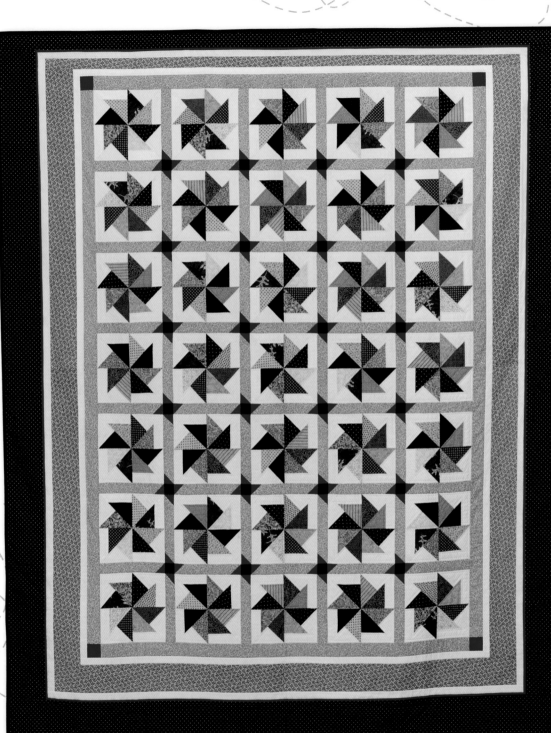

July

1
Monday

2
Tuesday

3
Wednesday

Independence Day (US)

4
Thursday

5
Friday

6
Saturday

7
Sunday

Blue-and-White Delight

Quiltmaker Sue Fitzgerald was inspired by her collection of blue and white china to make this scrap quilt, using rust-red accents to bring the design to life. This is just one of the incredible stash-busting patterns featured in Lynne Edwards' *Stash-Buster Quilts*. If your stash allows, you can easily increase the number of Spinning Pinwheel blocks to make a larger quilt.

JULY

M	T	W	T	F	S	S
1	2	3	4	5	6	7
8	9	10	11	12	13	14
15	16	17	18	19	20	21
22	23	24	25	26	27	28
29	30	31				

July

8
Monday

9
Tuesday

10
Wednesday

11
Thursday

12
Friday

13
Saturday

14
Sunday

Koi Waterfall

Panels printed with attractive scenes are a quick way to create an eye-catching quilt. Here a dynamic koi and waterfall panel has been edged with a braided border, made from rectangles of fabric sewn together at a 45 degree angle. *The Quilter's Bible* by Linda Clements is full of clever techniques for combining patchwork, appliqué and quilting to create striking designs.

			JULY			
M	T	W	T	F	S	S
1	2	3	4	5	6	7
8	9	10	11	12	13	14
15	16	17	18	19	20	21
22	23	24	25	26	27	28
29	30	31				

15
Monday

16
Tuesday

17
Wednesday

18
Thursday

19
Friday

20
Saturday

21
Sunday

Busy Bee Garden Cushion
Australian-based designer Lynette Anderson grew up in an English country village. She has drawn on her childhood memories to create the cottage-garden inspired designs in *Country Cottage Quilting*. This lovely project is a great way to practise the technique for a Busy Bee block before progressing on to make a full size bed quilt.

			JULY			
M	T	W	T	F	S	S
1	2	3	4	5	6	7
8	9	10	11	12	13	14
15	16	17	18	19	20	21
22	23	24	25	26	27	28
29	30	31				

22
Monday

23
Tuesday

24
Wednesday

25
Thursday

26
Friday

27
Saturday

28
Sunday

Sailing Boats

This Jelly Roll™ quilt uses a traditional Boat block, combined with a 16-patch block to create a bright and cheerful design for a little boy's bed. The good news is that after this quilt is completed you will still have half the strips remaining from your Jelly Roll™ to make a second design. *Two From One Jelly Roll Quilts* by Pam and Nicky Lintott has lots more ideas for making two different quilts from just one Jelly Roll™.

			JULY			
M	T	W	T	F	S	S
1	2	3	4	5	6	7
8	9	10	11	12	13	14
15	16	17	18	19	20	21
22	23	24	25	26	27	28
29	30	31				

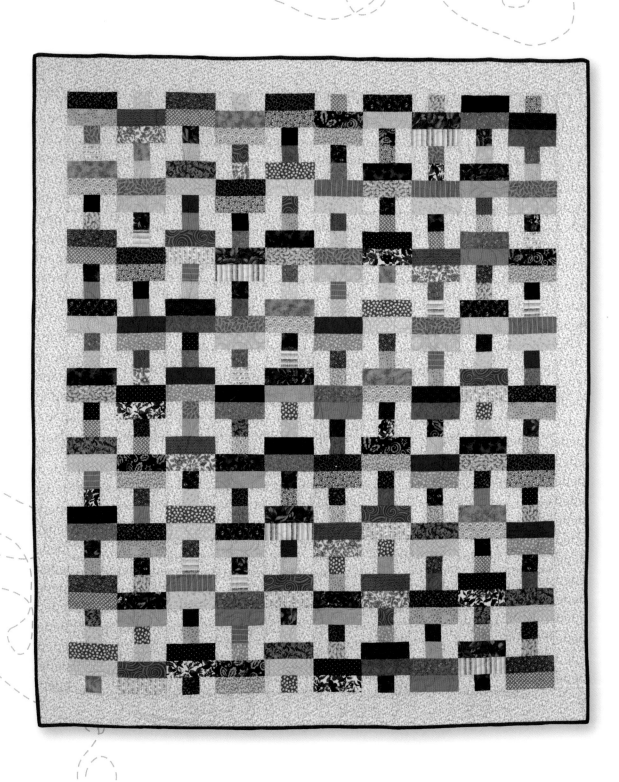

29
Monday

30
Tuesday

31
Wednesday

1
Thursday

2
Friday

3
Saturday

4
Sunday

Vertical Drop

The first Jelly Roll Challenge encouraged quilters of all abilities to design a quilt using just one Jelly Roll™. Shelagh Roberts' quilt was one of the 12 winning entries. She decided on a simple design that used fairly large pieces in order to showcase the material. The other prize-winning quilts can be seen in *Jelly Roll Inspirations* compiled by Pam and Nicky Lintott.

JULY

M	T	W	T	F	S	S
1	2	3	4	5	6	7
8	9	10	11	12	13	14
15	16	17	18	19	20	21
22	23	24	25	26	27	28
29	30	31				

August

5
Monday

6
Tuesday

7
Wednesday

8
Thursday

9
Friday

10
Saturday

11
Sunday

Galaxy of Stars and Scraps

Katharine Guerrier's book *Scrap Quilt Sensation* will inspire you
to utilize even your smallest fabric scrap to create a collection of
vividly colourful quilts. Just two Star blocks feature on this quilt
– the Friendship Star and the Eight-Pointed Star – yet by mixing the
fabrics in different ways, Katharine has created a veritable galaxy.

AUGUST

M	T	W	T	F	S	S
			1	2	3	4
5	6	7	8	9	10	11
12	13	14	15	16	17	18
19	20	21	22	23	24	25
26	27	28	29	30	31	

August

12
Monday

13
Tuesday

14
Wednesday

15
Thursday

16
Friday

17
Saturday

18
Sunday

AUGUST						
M	T	W	T	F	S	S
			1	2	3	4
5	6	7	8	9	10	11
12	13	14	15	16	17	18
19	20	21	22	23	24	25
26	27	28	29	30	31	

Best of Friends

It's Quilting Cats & Dogs by Lynette Anderson is an endearing collection of cat and dog designs, including this folk-art style quilt featuring Hugo (based on her own adorable dog) and his feathered friend Mr Bird.

August

19
Monday

20
Tuesday

21
Wednesday

22
Thursday

23
Friday

24
Saturday

25
Sunday

Daisy Table Setting

In *Folk Quilt Appliqué* Clare Kingslake shares her secrets for both hand and machine appliqué to create over 20 irresistible projects inspired by the naïve quality of folk art. This country kitchen table linen set features a table runner, table mat and coasters, appliquéd with a delightful little house hidden in a forest of daisies.

AUGUST

M	T	W	T	F	S	S
			1	2	3	4
5	6	7	8	9	10	11
12	13	14	15	16	17	18
19	20	21	22	23	24	25
26	27	28	29	30	31	

August/September

Summer Bank Holiday (UK)

26
Monday

27
Tuesday

28
Wednesday

29
Thursday

30
Friday

31
Saturday

Father's Day (Aus)

1
Sunday

Sweet Roses

The rose is perhaps the favourite of all garden flowers, and in *Floral Dimensions*, Pauline Ineson provides quilters with a masterclass on reproducing this popular plant in fabric. By using a lighter shade for the outer petals and a darker shade for the inner ones, she has perfectly captured the bloom of a summer rose. This is just one of 20 flowers re-created in 3D perfection in Pauline's book.

			AUGUST			
M	T	W	T	F	S	S
			1	2	3	4
5	6	7	8	9	10	11
12	13	14	15	16	17	18
19	20	21	22	23	24	25
26	27	28	29	30	31	

September

Labor Day (US)

2
Monday

3
Tuesday

4
Wednesday

5
Thursday

6
Friday

7
Saturday

8
Sunday

SEPTEMBER

M	T	W	T	F	S	S
						1
2	3	4	5	6	7	8
9	10	11	12	13	14	15
16	17	18	19	20	21	22
23	24	25	26	27	28	29
30						

Welcome Sampler

Making a sampler quilt is a perfect way to learn new skills and improve your techniques, and the small scale of a wall hanging is ideal for trying out pieced block designs new to you. This project from Mandy Shaw's *Quilt Yourself Gorgeous* makes great use of a fat eighth bundle with very little leftover.

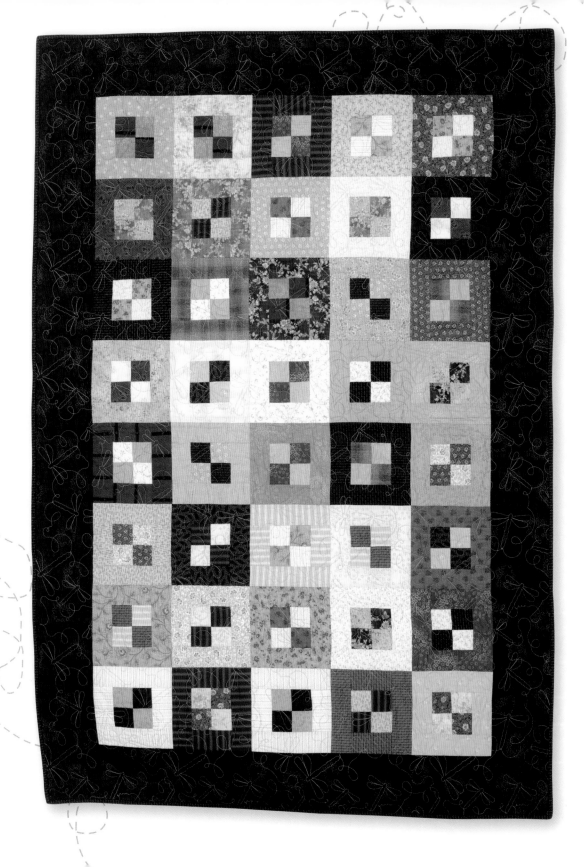

September

9
Monday

10
Tuesday

11
Wednesday

12
Thursday

13
Friday

14
Saturday

15
Sunday

Pandora's Box
The muted, earthy colours of Japanese taupes are subtle and sophisticated. This quilt, from Pam and Nicky Lintotts' *Jelly Roll Quilts*, would particularly complement a room that features natural materials, such as wood and leather. The black print border and quilted dragonflies all over add depth and texture.

SEPTEMBER

M	T	W	T	F	S	S
						1
2	3	4	5	6	7	8
9	10	11	12	13	14	15
16	17	18	19	20	21	22
23	24	25	26	27	28	29
30						

September

16
Monday

17
Tuesday

18
Wednesday

19
Thursday

20
Friday

21
Saturday

22
Sunday

Garden Trellis
This garden-inspired quilt, pieced by Pam and Nicky Lintott and long arm quilted by The Quilt Room, uses a soothing mix of country colours from a pretty country range from Blackbird Designs. It features in *Jelly Roll Quilts*.

		SEPTEMBER				
M	T	W	T	F	S	S
						1
2	3	4	5	6	7	8
9	10	11	12	13	14	15
16	17	18	19	20	21	22
23	24	25	26	27	28	29
30						

September

23
Monday

24
Tuesday

25
Wednesday

26
Thursday

27
Friday

28
Saturday

29
Sunday

Patchwork Kimono

Here the koi and waterfall panel (8th–14th July) has been used as the centrepiece for this stunning kimono quilt by Susan Briscoe (*Japanese Quilt Inspirations*). The sleeves are a patchwork of scraps and the background fabric has been chosen to contrast well so that the kimono shape stands out. The border print was selected from the same range as the koi panel.

SEPTEMBER

M	T	W	T	F	S	S
						1
2	3	4	5	6	7	8
9	10	11	12	13	14	15
16	17	18	19	20	21	22
23	24	25	26	27	28	29
30						

September/October

30
Monday

1
Tuesday

2
Wednesday

3
Thursday

4
Friday

5
Saturday

6
Sunday

OCTOBER						
M	T	W	T	F	S	S
	1	2	3	4	5	6
7	8	9	10	11	12	13
14	15	16	17	18	19	20
21	22	23	24	25	26	27
28	29	30	31			

Simple Squares

A quilt with a pattern of regular squares is a good choice for a newcomer to patchwork, and here you have two for the price of one, Four-Patch Squares and Squares and Diamonds. These designs are ideal for using up fabric scraps and were designed by colour expert Katharine Guerrier (*Scrap Quilt Sensation*).

October

7
Monday

8
Tuesday

9
Wednesday

10
Thursday

11
Friday

12
Saturday

13
Sunday

For Emma

This design by Jennifer Goldstein was awarded 3rd place in the 2011 Jelly Roll Dream Challenge. What Jennifer enjoyed most about this contest was the mathematical challenge of creating a quilt with minimal waste, so she utilized the remaining Jelly Roll™ strips in the appliqué border. All the prize-winning quilts can be seen in *Jelly Roll Dreams* compiled by Pam and Nicky Lintott.

OCTOBER

M	T	W	T	F	S	S
	1	2	3	4	5	6
7	8	9	10	11	12	13
14	15	16	17	18	19	20
21	22	23	24	25	26	27
28	29	30	31			

October

Columbus Day (US)

14
Monday

15
Tuesday

16
Wednesday

17
Thursday

18
Friday

19
Saturday

20
Sunday

Quilter's Briefcase

Susan Briscoe's patchwork bags are not only beautiful but incredibly useful too, addressing all your carrying needs. This portfolio from *21 Terrific Patchwork Bags* has been designed to keep all your quilting equipment safe at workshops. It can accommodate a cutting mat and has plenty of pockets too. The view from Susan's workroom window inspired the foundation-pieced side panels.

OCTOBER

M	T	W	T	F	S	S
	1	2	3	4	5	6
7	8	9	10	11	12	13
14	15	16	17	18	19	20
21	22	23	24	25	26	27
28	29	30	31			

October

21
Monday

22
Tuesday

23
Wednesday

24
Thursday

25
Friday

26
Saturday

27
Sunday

Make Your Mark

If you are ready to explore your creative side, *The Painted Quilt*
by Linda and Laura Kemshall will offer plenty of inspiration as
you find your own style. This photograph shows a detail from one
of Linda's quilts which combines simple piecing, appliqué and
printing with compressed sponge shapes.

			OCTOBER			
M	T	W	T	F	S	S
	1	2	3	4	5	6
7	8	9	10	11	12	13
14	15	16	17	18	19	20
21	22	23	24	25	26	27
28	29	30	31			

28
Monday

29
Tuesday

30
Wednesday

Halloween

31
Thursday

1
Friday

2
Saturday

3
Sunday

Big and Bold Sampler

Each of the 10 quilts featured in *Jelly Roll Sampler Quilts* by Pam
and Nicky Lintott is made from just one Jelly Roll™. This stunning
quilt is made up of five large blocks (Japanese Star, Chequered Star,
Carpenter's Wheel, Blackford Beauty and Railroad Crossing) linked
together with an easy connector block. The book features 55 fabulous
block designs for making your own unique sampler quilts.

OCTOBER

M	T	W	T	F	S	S
	1	2	3	4	5	6
7	8	9	10	11	12	13
14	15	16	17	18	19	20
21	22	23	24	25	26	27
28	29	30	31			

November

4
Monday

5
Tuesday

6
Wednesday

7
Thursday

8
Friday

9
Saturday

10
Sunday

Drying in the Breeze
This quilt, from Clare Kingslake's *Folk Quilt Appliqué* depicts a moment in time in a lovely rural setting – a country house, plump geese in the field and two delightful little quilts drying in the breeze on a washing line in the orchard.

NOVEMBER

M	T	W	T	F	S	S
				1	2	3
4	5	6	7	8	9	10
11	12	13	14	15	16	17
18	19	20	21	22	23	24
25	26	27	28	29	30	

November

Veterans Day (US)

11
Monday

12
Tuesday

13
Wednesday

14
Thursday

15
Friday

16
Saturday

17
Sunday

Igeta (Well-Curb)
The patchwork block on this quilt design is inspired by the *kanji* character *igeta* which looks just like what it says, the criss-crossed timbers known as well-curbs once seen all over Japan. These grilles protected the unwary from tumbling into an open well head. All the quilts that feature in Susan Briscoe's *Japanese Quilt Inspirations* have been based on traditional Japanese sources.

NOVEMBER						
M	T	W	T	F	S	S
				1	2	3
4	5	6	7	8	9	10
11	12	13	14	15	16	17
18	19	20	21	22	23	24
25	26	27	28	29	30	

November

18
Monday

19
Tuesday

20
Wednesday

21
Thursday

22
Friday

23
Saturday

24
Sunday

Crimson Wave

This lap quilt by quiltmaker Yvonne Dawson is a fine example of a Bargello quilt. The design looks complex but it is easily made from strips of different fabrics stitched together before being cut into pieces and rearranged to create the illusion of curves or flame-like points. It is a great way to use up an excess stash of red fabrics and can be found in Lynne Edwards' *Stash-Buster Quilts*.

NOVEMBER

M	T	W	T	F	S	S
				1	2	3
4	5	6	7	8	9	10
11	12	13	14	15	16	17
18	19	20	21	22	23	24
25	26	27	28	29	30	

25
Monday

26
Tuesday

27
Wednesday

Thanksgiving (US)

28
Thursday

29
Friday

30
Saturday

1
Sunday

Candy Heart

This heart design by Pamela Boatright, one of the finalists in the 2009 Jelly Roll Challenge competiton, was designed as a shop sample to help sell a new line of jelly rolls in her local quilt shop in Coos Bay, Oregon. Pamela was persuaded to enter the quilting competition by a friend – her quilt was selected by Pam and Nicky Lintott to appear in *Jelly Roll Inspirations*.

			NOVEMBER			
M	T	W	T	F	S	S
				1	2	3
4	5	6	7	8	9	10
11	12	13	14	15	16	17
18	19	20	21	22	23	24
25	26	27	28	29	30	

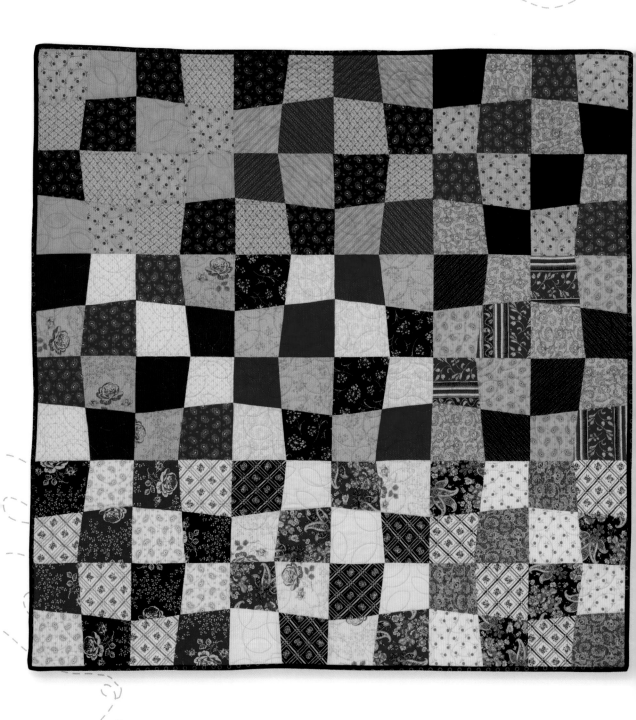

December

2
Monday

3
Tuesday

4
Wednesday

5
Thursday

6
Friday

7
Saturday

8
Sunday

Tipsy Tumblers

More Layer Cake, Jelly Roll & Charm Quilts is full of quilts
that have been created using pre-cut fabrics, packed up
and ready to sew. This topsy turvy quilt, from Pam and Nicky
Linott, is great for showcasing fabrics because the blocks
are large, leaving the fabrics to speak for themselves!

DECEMBER

M	T	W	T	F	S	S
						1
2	3	4	5	6	7	8
9	10	11	12	13	14	15
16	17	18	19	20	21	22
23	24	25	26	27	28	29
30	31					

December

Kasuri Throw

This lovely throw features in *Japanese Sashiko Inspirations* by Susan Briscoe. The colour depth of the indigo blue *tsumugi* cotton, woven with blue threads on a black warp, makes a striking contrast with the cream calico patchwork. The simply-pieced *Igeta* (Well-Curb) blocks alternate with sashiko picture motifs, which include a koi, castle, floral circle and the Japanese character for good fortune.

DECEMBER

M	T	W	T	F	S	S
						1
2	3	4	5	6	7	8
9	10	11	12	13	14	15
16	17	18	19	20	21	22
23	24	25	26	27	28	29
30	31					

December

16
Monday

17
Tuesday

18
Wednesday

19
Thursday

20
Friday

21
Saturday

22
Sunday

Bird and Feathers

In *The Painted Quilt*, Laura and Linda Kemshall illustrate how their textile ideas are translated from sketchbook to quilt often over several pieces of work. This design is the first of a series of landscape-inspired hangings, each strip-pieced with a limited colour palette, then subjected to different painting techniques to see how their basic appearance could be changed.

DECEMBER

M	T	W	T	F	S	S
						1
2	3	4	5	6	7	8
9	10	11	12	13	14	15
16	17	18	19	20	21	22
23	24	25	26	27	28	29
30	31					

December

23
Monday

24
Tuesday

Christmas Day

25
Wednesday

Boxing Day (UK, Aus)

26
Thursday

27
Friday

28
Saturday

29
Sunday

Log Cabin Hidden Stars

Jelly Roll Quilts by Pam and Nicky Lintott is the perfect guide to making the most of these pre-cut strips of fabric, and each of the featured quilts can be made using just one Jelly Roll™. When thinking of patterns using strips, the Log Cabin block comes immediately to mind, and here the traditional design has been given an extra lift with the addition of the stars. This makes the perfect festive quilt when made up in sumptuous country reds and greens.

DECEMBER

M	T	W	T	F	S	S
						1
2	3	4	5	6	7	8
9	10	11	12	13	14	15
16	17	18	19	20	21	22
23	24	25	26	27	28	29
30	31					

December /January

30
Monday

31
Tuesday

New Year's Day

1
Wednesday

2
Thursday

3
Friday

4
Saturday

5
Sunday

Matsuri Festival

This version of the Igeta quilt (11th–17th November) uses a vibrant black and red colour scheme and the vivid colour choice has been inspired by the traditional *happi* jackets – half red and half black – worn by dancers and musicians at Japanese festivals. *Japanese Quilt Inspirations* by Susan Briscoe is packed with designs inspired by the style and culture of this fascinating country.

JANUARY

M	T	W	T	F	S	S
		1	2	3	4	5
6	7	8	9	10	11	12
13	14	15	16	17	18	19
20	21	22	23	24	25	26
27	28	29	30	31		

Useful Information

It is hoped that the quilt photographs featured in this diary have inspired you to take your own quilt skills further. Wherever you are located, there are bound to be opportunities for you to see other quilters' work and to share your love of this amazing textile art. Use the following information to help you find out what is going on near you.

UK
Organizations

The Quilters' Guild of the British Isles is an independent registered educational charity with over 7,000 members. **www.quiltersguild.org.uk**

Exhibitions

The Festival of Quilts
Organized by Creative Exhibitions Ltd with the support of the Quilters Guild of the British Isles, this is the largest quilt show in Europe with over 30,000 visitors each year. A four-day show held in August at the National Exhibition Centre, Birmingham, it has over 1,000 competition quilts on display, as well as galleries from leading international quilt artists and groups. There are over 300 exhibitors selling specialist patchwork and quilting supplies, plus hundreds of masterclasses, workshops and lectures.
www.twistedthread.com

Quilts UK
The organizers of this exhibition, Grosvenor Shows Ltd, hold several patchwork and quilting exhibitions nationally each year. The largest of these is Quilts UK held in May at the Three Counties Showground in the beautiful Malvern Hills in Worcestershire. The longest established show in the UK, it attracts over 9,000 visitors annually. It is an open competitive show with over 400 quilts on display and 150 trade stands.
www.grosvenorexhibitions.co.uk

The National Quilt Championships
An open competitive quilt show held at Sandown Park in June attracting over 5,000 visitors. Over 400 quilts are on display, including features from well-known artists from the UK and overseas, incorporating a mix of traditional and contemporary quilts.
www.grosvenorexhibitions.co.uk

Spring and Autumn Quilt Festivals
A number of smaller, local quilt shows are also organized by Grosvenor Shows Ltd. Locations include: Ardingly, Chilford, Edinburg, Exeter, Maidstone and Malvern.
www.grosvenorexhibitions.co.uk

Quiltfest
Quiltfest's aim is to showcase the cutting edge of textile design and making, and to enable quiltmakers in Wales and the Northwest of England to see work that may not normally be exhibited in the region. It is an annual show held in February at Llangollen Museum and Art Gallery.
www.quiltfest.org.uk

USA
Organizations

American Quilter's Society (AQS)
The aim of the AQS is to provide a forum for quilters of all skill levels to expand their horizons in quiltmaking, design, self-expression and quilt collecting. It publishes books and magazines, has product offers, and runs quilt shows and contests, workshops and other activities.
www.americanquilter.com

The International Quilting Association (IQA)
The IQA is a non-profit organization dedicated to the preservation of the art of quilting, the attainment of public recognition for quilting as an art form, and the advancement of the state of the art throughout the world. Founded in 1979, it supports many quilting projects and activities, and organizes two annual Judged Shows of members' work exhibited at the International Quilt Markets and Festivals held throughout the year.
www.quilts.com

Exhibitions

American Quilter's Society Quilt Shows
The AQS organizes a number of quilt shows annually and in 2013 these will be held in Paducah, Kentucky (April), Grand Rapids, Michigan (August), and Des Moines, Iowa (October).
www.americanquilter.com

The International Quilting Association Quilt Shows
Quilts, Inc., the IQA's exhibiton arm, holds three consumer shows (Quilt Festival) and two trade shows (Quilt Market) annually.
www.quilts.com

Sisters Outdoor Quilt Show
This is the largest outdoor quilt show in the world with over 12,500 attendees and is held on the second Saturday of July in Sisters, Oregon.
www.sistersoutdoorquiltshow.org

The Mancuso Quilt Shows
Mancuso Show Management, run by brothers David and Peter Mancuso, promotes seven major national and international quilting and textile arts festivals held across the USA.
www.quiltfest.com

CANADA
Organizations

Canadian Quilters' Association
Formed in 1981, the aims and objectives of the Canadian Quilters' Association are: to promote a greater understanding, appreciation, and knowledge of the art, techniques, and heritage of patchwork, appliqué, and quilting; to promote the highest standards of workmanship and design in both traditional and innovative work; and to foster cooperation and sharing among quiltmakers. There are a number of Canadian Quilters' Association sponsored events including the National Juried Show (NJS), Canada's most prestigious quilt show.
www.canadianquilter.com

AUSTRALIA
Organizations

The Quilters' Guild of NSW
A Sydney-based organization which aims to promote the art and craft of patchwork and quilting. Membership is open to anyone with an interest in the craft, from the beginner to the professional, and it has over 1,000 members.
www.quiltersguildnsw.com

Quilters' Guild of South Australia
This organization has over 500 individual guild members with over 100 city and country groups now affiliated with the guild.
www.saquilters.org.au

Exhibitions

Australia's No.1 Craft and Quilt Fairs
Expertise Events run several craft and quilting fairs in Australia (Perth, Sydney, Launceston – Tasmania, Melbourne, Canberra, Brisbane, Adelaide) and New Zealand (Hamilton).
www.craftfair.com.au

The Australasian Quilt Convention (AQC)
Held in Melbourne, this is Australia's largest annual quilt-dedicated event, incorporating classes and lectures with highly skilled tutors, much-anticipated social events, a shopping market plus exhibitor workshops and exclusive quilt displays. It brings together thousands of quilters from all over Australia and around the world.
www.aqc.com.au

NEW ZEALAND
Organizations

Aotearoa National Association of New Zealand Quilters
Formed in 1994 as the National Association of New Zealand Quilters (NANZQ) the principle objective is to promote and lead the development of patchwork, quilting and textile artists within New Zealand.
www.aotearoaquilters.co.nz

Exhibitions

Taupo Symposium 2013 Fabric Art Festival
The 15th National Patchwork and Quilting Symposium will be held on 18th–23rd July on the shores of Lake Taupo in North Island. Up to 1,500 New Zealand and overseas participants will be involved, attending a wide range of classes and workshops, lectures, merchants' markets and exhibitions, among other activities. There are over 50 classes a day, tutored by well-known overseas and national tutors.
www.tauposymposium.co.nz

More About the Quilts

The quilts included in the *Quilter's Desk Diary 2013* have all been selected from the great range of patchwork and quilting books published by David & Charles. If you would like to find out more about any of the quilt designs featured, why not treat yourself to a few of these great books. For more information about these and other high quality craft books visit: **www.rucraft.co.uk**

21 Terrific Patchwork Bags
Susan Briscoe

ISBN-13: 978-0-7153-1443-2

This collection of 21 essential bags for every occasion allows you to explore a wealth of different patchwork techniques, and is packed with ideas for customizing the designs to suit your needs.

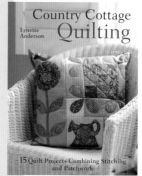

Country Cottage Quilting
Lynette Anderson

ISBN-13: 978-1-4463-0039-8

The country cottage garden provides the inspiration for this collection of beautiful quilting and stitchery designs, featuring wall quilts, bags, cushion covers, all in Lynette's distinctive style.

The Essential Sampler Quilt Book
Lynne Edwards

ISBN-13: 978-0-7153-3613-7

Masterclass instruction from the sampler quilt expert for making 40 pieced blocks using both hand and machine techniques, with a wealth of quilt photographs to inspire colour and fabric choices.

Folk Quilt Appliqué
Clare Kingslake

ISBN-13: 978-0-7153-3826-1

Drawing on a palette of soft, country colours, Clare Kingslake presents a collection of 20 irresistible projects in a her quirky folk style, using both hand and machine appliqué techniques.

Floral Dimensions
Pauline Ineson

ISBN-13: 978-1-4463-0181-4

Features 20 gorgeous dimensional flowers cleverly manipulated in fabric, including the daffodil, marigold, rose and tulip, and derived from the author's incredible multi-award winning quilt.

It's Quilting Cats & Dogs
Lynette Anderson

ISBN-13: 978-0-7153-3757-8

If you like cats and dogs, you'll love these 17 great projects. The heart-warming designs combine simple but stunning hand stitchery with traditional patchwork and quilting techniques.

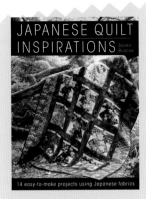

Japanese Quilt Inspirations
Susan Briscoe

ISBN-13: 978-0-7153-3827-8

Ten stunning quilt designs that make clever use of fabric favourites such as fat quarters, strip rolls and feature panels, as well as kimono widths and furoshiki (wrapping cloths).

Japanese Sashiko Inspirations
Susan Briscoe

ISBN-13: 978-0-7153-2641-4

Discover sashiko, the Japanese method of decorative stitching to create striking patterns on fabric with lines of simple running stitch. Bring a touch of the Orient to your home with over 25 projects to choose from.

Jelly Roll Dreams
Pam & Nicky Lintott

ISBN-13: 978-1-4463-0040-4

A stunning showcase for the 12 winning quilts from the 2011 Jelly Roll Dream Challenge, each made from just one Jelly Roll™, with variations provided by Pam & Nicky Lintott.

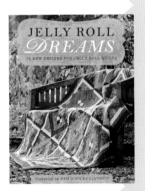

Jelly Roll Inspirations
Pam & Nicky Lintott

ISBN-13: 978-0-7153-3311-2

The aim of the Jelly Roll Challenge competition was to find the best and most creative use of just one jelly roll. Gathered here are the 12 fabulous winning entries, with step-by-step instructions and a colour variation on each.

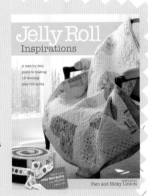

Jelly Roll Quilts
Pam & Nicky Lintott

ISBN-13: 978-0-7153-2863-7

Jelly Roll Quilts was the first book on the market to show the best ways to use these desirable and labour-saving fabric packs consisting of 2½ inch strips of colour co-ordinated fabric. There are 17 designs, each of which can be made from just one roll.

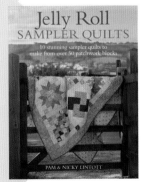

Jelly Roll Sampler Quilts
Pam & Nicky Lintott

ISBN-13: 978-0-7153-3844-5

Making a sampler quilt featuring as many different patchwork blocks as possible is every quilter's dream. All you jelly roll lovers out there, make the dream come true.

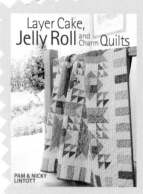

Layer Cake, Jelly Roll and Charm Quilts
Pam & Nicky Lintott

ISBN-13: 978-0-7153-3208-5

Seventeen beautiful projects, from lap quilts to bed quilts, show you how to get the most from irresistible pre-cut fabric bundles.

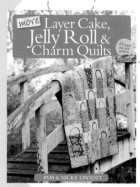

More Layer Cake, Jelly Roll & Charm Quilts
Pam & Nicky Lintott

ISBN-13: 978-0-7153-3898-8

A second helping of 14 brand new quilt designs to help quilters get the most from favourite pre-cut fabric bundles, for quilts that are quick to piece and a joy to make.

The Painted Quilt
Linda & Laura Kemshall

ISBN-13: 978-0-7153-2450-9

This inspirational book demystifies the process of colouring cloth by various means including fabric paints, pastels, dyes, bleaches and transfers. Simple techniques are combined to produce complex textile surfaces, all easily explained step by step.

Quilt a Gift
Barri Sue Gaudet

ISBN-13: 978-0-7153-3282-5

Whether you have a week, a day, or just a couple of hours to stitch it, you'll find the perfect gift idea here for family or friends, whatever the occasion.

Quilt a Gift for Little Ones
Barri Sue Gaudet

ISBN-13: 978-0-7153-3866-7

Over 20 gorgeous gifts to make for the new arrival from bunting and blankets to cot quilts and comforters. With themes ranging from bunnies to bears, choose to make a quick project or an heirloom treasure.

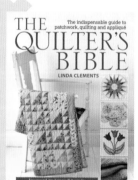

The Quilter's Bible
Lin Clements

ISBN-13: 978-0-7153-3626-7

This is the ultimate quilter's companion to over 220 patchwork, quilting and appliqué techniques, and it is illustrated with more than 800 colour diagrams.

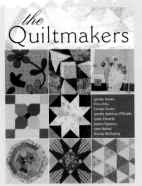

The Quiltmakers
Consultant Editor:
Pam Lintott

ISBN-13: 978-0-7153-3173-6

A unique opportunity to take eight masterclasses from some of the very best quilters in the world, without ever leaving home. Topics include creating perspective, perfect piecing, and inspired fabric collage.

Quilt Yourself Gorgeous
Mandy Shaw

ISBN-13: 978-0-7153-2830-9

Mandy has a fresh approach to quilting with an emphasis on fun, fast results and fabulous quilts. She includes 20 brilliant projects that have plenty of wow factor, but won't take a lifetime to complete.

Scrap Quilt Sensation
Katharine Guerrier

ISBN-13: 978-0-7153-2452-3

A sumptuous collection of scrap quilts with a contemporary twist on traditional designs. Twelve step-by-step projects, with in-depth advice on selecting the right fabrics from your stash and how to combine them for best effect.

Stash-Buster Quilts
Lynne Edwards

ISBN-13: 978-0-7153-2463-2

Lynne Edwards continues her campaign to help you reduce your fabric collection leaving you free to buy more. Twenty scrap quilts are described, as well as a selection of smaller projects, from bags to soft toys, to ensure every last scrap is used up.

Stitch at Home
Mandy Shaw

ISBN-13: 978-1-4463-0168-5

Get stitching with 20 gorgeous embroidery and appliqué projects for your home, your garden and your loved ones! Combining appliqué, embroidery, patchwork, quilting and sewing.

Two from One Jelly Roll Quilts
Pam & Nicky Lintott

ISBN-13: 978-0-7153-3756-1

Learn how to make two different quilts using just one jelly roll – half the fabric, twice the inspiration. It features 18 patterns to help you make your fabric go further.

More About the Quiltmakers

The quilt designs featured in *The Quilter's Desk Diary 2013* showcase the talents of some of the world's most respected and creative quiltmakers. The names of those whose work is included are listed below.

Lynette Anderson was born in Dorset, England and moved to Australia in 1990 where she founded The Patchwork Angel store in 1997. Lynette is now focussed full time on designing her extensive pattern range, as well as fabrics for Henry Glass & Co. www.lynetteandersondesigns.typepad.com

Pamela Boatright was one of the finalists in the 2009 Jelly Roll Challenge. Her quilt now features as a project in *Jelly Roll Inspirations*.

Susan Briscoe was introduced to sashiko while teaching English in Japan. Susan's sashiko designs have been published in *Popular Patchwork*, *British Patchwork & Quilting* and *Fabrications*, and she has written over ten books on quilting. www.susanbriscoe.co.uk

Linda Clements has been a specialist craft editor for many years and is the author of best-selling *The Quilter's Bible*. Passionate about quilting, she has learnt and developed her skills by working with some of the best quilting teachers.

Laura Coons is the winner of the 2011 Jelly Roll Dream Challenge. Her quilt, Garden Walk, appears as a project and on the front cover of *Jelly Roll Dreams*.

Paula Diggle was one of the finalists in the 2009 Jelly Roll Challenge. Her quilt now features as a project in *Jelly Roll Inspirations*.

Lynne Edwards specializes in sampler quilts and the cathedral window technique. She has been the recipient of many prestigious awards including the Jewel Pearce Patterson Scholarship for International Quilt Teachers and the Amy Emms Memorial Trophy. In 2008 she was awarded an MBE for services to Arts and Crafts.

Joanna Figueroa is a talented designer and quiltmaker and founder of Fig Tree & Co. Joanna designs the gorgeous Fig Tree fabrics for Moda fabrics. She has published over 100 quilting, sewing and children's patterns and design booklets, and travels regularly for national and international teaching engagements and seminars. www.figtreeandco.com

Barri Sue Gaudet began her own pattern company, Bareroots, in 1999 and has enjoyed creating original designs of all kinds ever since. She travels widely to teach, and also runs a stitchery and knitting shop in Bishop, California named Sierra Cottons & Wools. www.bareroots.com

Jennifer Golstein won third prize in the 2011 Jelly Roll Dream Challenge. Her beautiful Emma's Quilt now features as a project in *Jelly Roll Dreams*.

Katharine Guerrier is the author of numerous books including *Quilting from Start to Finish* and *Scrap Quilt Sensation*. She also contributes regularly to several quilting magazines with articles, projects and reviews. www.katharineguerrier.com

Claire Hepworth won fourth prize in the 2011 Jelly Roll Dream Challenge. Her Lovin' That Muffin Quilt now features as a project in *Jelly Roll Dreams*.

Pauline Ineson is an award-winning quilter who specializes in machine sewing and appliqué techniques. She has taught machine sewing courses for over 10 years, and these include the Heirloom Quilt and the Appliqué Quilt courses. www.paulineineson.co.uk

Clare Kingslake is an expert in appliqué techniques and exquisite handwork. Her popular designs have been featured in magazines in the UK and France. www.clarespatterns.co.uk

Laura Kemshall and Linda Kemshall are renowned for their innovative approach to textiles as well as their City & Guilds creative courses through their fully accredited online centre. They have exhibited at many prestigious events all over the world to critical acclaim, and won several major awards for innovative design, use of colour and machine appliqué and quilting. Laura also designs and produces an exclusive range of products available through her online DesignMatters Store. www.lindakemshall.com

Pam Lintott and **Nicky Lintott** run The Quilt Room in Dorking, Surrey. Pam's first book, *The Quilt Room*, was a compilation of work from the very best patchworkers. Pam has also written several books with Nicky including the phenomenally successful *Jelly Roll Quilts*. An excellent quilter in her own right, Nicky's focus is on developing the longarm quilting business. www.quiltroom.co.uk

Shelagh Roberts was one of the finalists in the 2009 Jelly Roll Challenge. Her colourful Vertical Drop quilt now features as a project in *Jelly Roll Inspirations*.

Mandy Shaw runs Dandelion Designs, a craft design and kit company. Her work has featured on several TV programmes including *Kirstie's Homemade Christmas* (Channel 4), and she has written for *Popular Patchwork*, *Homespun* and *Fabrications* magazines. She teaches all over the country and her fast, trendy, no-fuss approach to patchwork makes her classes consistently popular. www.dandeliondesigns.co.uk

Angelika Sins won second prize in the Jelly Roll Dream Challenge 2011. Her quilt now features as a project in *Jelly Roll Dreams*.

A DAVID & CHARLES BOOK
© F&W Media International, Ltd 2012

David & Charles is an imprint of F&W Media International, Ltd
Brunel House, Forde Close, Newton Abbot, TQ12 4PU, UK

F&W Media International, Ltd is a subsidiary of F+W Media, Inc
10151 Carver Road, Cincinnati OH45242, USA

Text, layout and photography © F&W Media International, Ltd 2012

First published in the UK and USA in 2012

A catalogue record for this book is available from the British Library.

ISBN-13: 978-1-4463-0259-0 hardback
ISBN-10: 1-4463-0259-8 hardback

Printed in China by Toppan Leefung Printing Limited for:
F&W Media International, Ltd
Brunel House, Forde Close, Newton Abbot, TQ12 4PU, UK

Front cover quilt by Pam & Nicky Lintott photographed by Lorna Yabsley
Back cover quilt by Jill Randel photographed by Lorna Yabsley

F+W Media publishes high quality books on a wide range of subjects.
For more great book ideas visit: www.rucraft.co.uk